ALTERNATIVE ENERGY

HYDROELECTRIC ENERGY

by Terry Catasús Jennings

Content Consultant
Nadipuram Prasad
Associate Professor, Klipsch School of
Electrical and Computer Engineering
New Mexico State University

Core Library

An Imprint of Abdo Publishing
abdopublishing.com

abdopublishing.com

Published by Abdo Publishing, a division of ABDO, PO Box 398166, Minneapolis, Minnesota 55439. Copyright © 2017 by Abdo Consulting Group, Inc. International copyrights reserved in all countries. No part of this book may be reproduced in any form without written permission from the publisher. Core Library™ is a trademark and logo of Abdo Publishing.

Printed in the United States of America, North Mankato, Minnesota
082016
012017

THIS BOOK CONTAINS
RECYCLED MATERIALS

Cover Photo: Chaiyagorn Phermphoon
Interior Photos: Chaiyagorn Phermphoon, 1; Shutterstock Images, 4, 40; Sheila Terry/Science Source, 7, 12; Stock Montage/Getty Images, 15; Alfred T. Palmer/Library of Congress, 17; Andrew Zarivny/Shutterstock Images, 19, 43; Stefano Ember/Shutterstock Images, 22, 45; Mark Williamson/Science Source, 25; Red Line Editorial, 27; Darren Poore/DK Images, 29; Flaxphotos/Shutterstock Images, 31; Songquan Deng/Shutterstock Images, 34; Dmitry Naumov/ Shutterstock Images, 36; Dana Jensen/The Day/AP Images, 39

Editor: Arnold Ringstad
Series Designer: Nikki Farinella

Publisher's Cataloging-in-Publication Data

Names: Jennings, Terry Catasús, author.
Title: Hydroelectric energy / by Terry Catasús Jennings.
Description: Minneapolis, MN : Abdo Publishing, 2017. | Series: Alternative
     energy | Includes bibliographical references and index.
Identifiers: LCCN 2016945433 | ISBN 9781680784558 (lib. bdg.) |
     ISBN 9781680798401 (ebook)
Subjects: LCSH: Water power--Juvenile literature. | Renewable energy
     sources--Juvenile literature.
Classification: DDC 621.31--dc23
LC record available at http://lccn.loc.gov/2016945433

CONTENTS

CHAPTER ONE

WHAT IS HYDROELECTRIC POWER?

It's a hot afternoon in California. People are beginning to leave their offices for the day. When they get home, many of them will turn on their air conditioners. Huge amounts of electricity will be needed.

At a nearby river, workers at a hydroelectric plant spring into action. A dam blocks the river, forming an artificial lake called a reservoir. Doors in the dam

Hydroelectric plants turn the rushing motion of falling water into electricity.

lift, and water begins to rush through. It careens into the plant. The water crashes into turbines, making the blades spin. Generators turn this spinning motion into electricity. In seconds, this electricity is ready to make the city's air conditioners hum. They will run on hydroelectric power.

Hydro is Greek for *water*. Hydroelectric plants convert the energy of falling water into electricity. They use water from rivers and streams. Hydroelectricity does not pollute the environment. It is a clean, reliable way to generate electricity.

Fueling Our Lives

Before the 1700s, taking advantage of flowing water was the only way to do work without human or animal power. People used water mills to grind grains and do other simple tasks. In the late 1700s, the industrial revolution saw the invention of the steam engine. The world began to use fossil fuels such as oil, coal, and natural gas to power these engines.

Steam engines powered the industrial revolution.

Fossil fuels are found underground. They must be brought up. Digging or pumping for these fuels can harm the environment. Then they must be burned to make electricity. Burning them sends harmful gases into the air. These gases cause climate change, the gradual warming of the planet over time. Additionally, a limited amount of these fuels is available. Eventually they will run out. For these reasons, people are looking to alternative energy sources that are clean and renewable. Hydroelectricity is one of these sources.

Hydroelectric power is used more than any other alternative energy source. In 2015 hydropower provided approximately 6 percent of all the electricity used

Energy Sources

In 2015 approximately 67 percent of the United States' electricity came from fossil fuels. Almost all of this was from coal and natural gas. Approximately 20 percent of the nation's power came from nuclear power plants. The remaining 13 percent came from various alternative energy sources. These included hydropower, solar power, and wind power.

in the United States. It is a reliable source of energy. It works on calm days when wind power doesn't work. It works on cloudy days when solar power can't work. Reservoirs store water for later use similar to the way a battery stores power. Workers at hydroelectric plants can release this water into the turbines to quickly produce more electricity. Waterpower can be generated on rivers in big cities. It can also bring inexpensive electricity to remote places. It can make life better for people in rural areas.

The Power Grid

Electricity travels on wires from power plants to homes. Some wires are aboveground. Others are buried underground. Together, all these wires make up the power grid. Power plants feed electricity into the grid. The grid allows hydropower to back up other types of power plants. When more electricity is needed, extra hydropower can be fed into the grid.

Hydropower reservoirs have many other uses. The artificial lakes provide a place to enjoy water sports.

Their water can be used to water crops. And the dams can be used to prevent harmful floods.

Making It Even Better

Hydropower is a useful source of energy. But it is not perfect. When a dam forms a reservoir, people living in the area of the reservoir must move away. Towns disappear. The change to the local environment can harm plants and animals. Dams prevent fish from swimming freely up the river.

Despite these problems, hydroelectric power remains one of today's most promising technologies. Scientists are working to overcome its issues and make it even better. Hydroelectricity is likely to become one of the most important parts of our energy future.

In 1999 inventor Robert Komarechka patented a way to generate hydroelectricity inside a person's shoe. In his patent application, he described how the invention would work:

> *A hydroelectric generator assembly for use in footwear includes a pair of fluid filled sacs contained in the sole of the footwear. The sacs are connected by conduits whereby, when the footwear is used for walking, fluid is transferred between the sacs, via the conduits. A turbine positioned between the conduits is rotated by the moving fluid thereby resulting in the generation of electricity.*

> *Source: "Footwear with Hydroelectric Generator Assembly." Google Patents. Google Patents, n.d. Web. Accessed April 15, 2016.*

Consider Your Audience

How is the idea for the hydropower shoe similar to the description of hydroelectric plants in Chapter One? How is it different? What uses do you see for this invention? Write a blog post telling your principal or friends about it.

CHAPTER TWO

THE OLDEST TYPE OF POWER

Humans have used waterpower for more than 5,000 years. The ancient Egyptians, Chinese, Greeks, and Romans all used water wheels to grind grains. Flowing water would spin a wheel, and the wheel would be attached to a shaft or gears. This motion would turn a stone, which would grind grain into flour. By 1086 CE, England had about 6,000 water mills. The force of falling water was the top

Water wheels have been in use since ancient times.

source of mechanical power until the invention of the steam engine.

By the time of the industrial revolution, sawmills and textile mills dotted riverbanks. People moved to cities. But waterpower could not meet the new need for energy. It could only be generated next to a river or stream. It needed a place where water fell. Coal-fired steam engines could be built anywhere. They could be used to make machines run. These engines powered the world's growing cities.

Lights!

English scientist Michael Faraday developed the generator in 1831. A generator turns motion into electricity. It can be a coil of wire that spins inside a magnetic field. It may also be a magnet that spins inside a coil of wire.

Thomas Edison invented the light bulb in 1879. The first lights were powered by water. A water wheel turned a generator to power lights in Grand Rapids, Michigan. The wheel at a flour mill powered

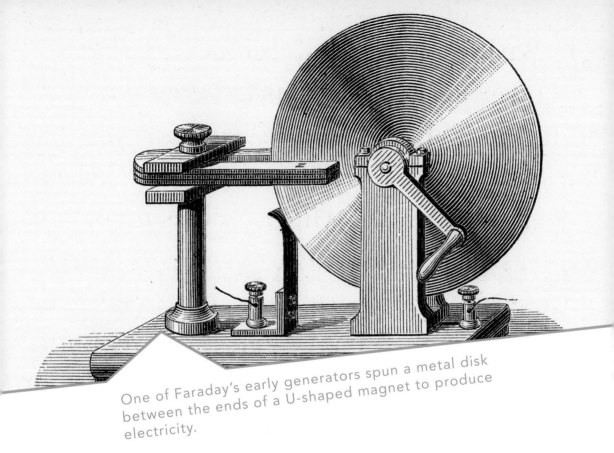

One of Faraday's early generators spun a metal disk between the ends of a U-shaped magnet to produce electricity.

street lights in Niagara Falls, New York. The first hydroelectric power plant was built in 1882. It was built in Appleton, Wisconsin. It powered lights in a private home and two paper mills.

Electric Power Grows

Serbian-American inventor Nikola Tesla worked on ways to send electricity over long distances. He also invented an electric motor in 1887. His inventions made electricity a more flexible source of power.

It could be used for more than lights. Demand for power boomed. For the first time, a dam was built just to generate electricity. It was built in Redlands, California.

Electricity for All

In the 1930s, the Great Depression gripped the United States. Millions of people became poor and hungry. Jobs were scarce. Many Americans struggled to survive.

The Great Depression hit rural areas especially hard. People in these places had no electricity. Farmers could not afford to build power lines all the way out to their farms.

President Franklin Roosevelt worked to bring electricity to these areas. In 1933 he created the Tennessee Valley Authority (TVA). It built dams and power plants in the Tennessee Valley. It brought electricity to rural communities. It also brought jobs.

The government also built great dams in the West. Hoover Dam was completed in 1936. It is built

TVA workers build a dam in Tennessee in 1942.

across the Colorado River on the border of Arizona and Nevada. The Grand Coulee Dam in Washington opened in 1942. Hydroelectric plants at these dams still provide power to millions of people. But the country's hunger for power during this time was huge. Power companies met most of this need with fossil fuel power plants.

World War II

In World War II (1939–1945), the Allies fought against the Axis powers. The Allies included the United States, the United Kingdom, and the Soviet Union. The Axis powers

---

Before the TVA

Life without electricity in the Tennessee Valley was harsh. People used a fossil fuel called kerosene for lighting. There was no power to pump water out of wells, so farmers carried water to their homes in buckets. No running water also meant no indoor bathrooms. People stored their food in iceboxes, rather than refrigerators. They could keep their food cold only when they had a fresh block of ice. All washing was done by hand, and there were no radios. President Roosevelt and the TVA changed all that by bringing electricity to these rural areas.

Hoover Dam is one of the world's most famous dams.

included Germany, Italy, and Japan. The Allies needed planes, tanks, and ships. But the United Kingdom did not have money to make goods needed for war. It did not have enough factories. It fell to the United States to do the job. Making weapons for the Allies created a new demand for electricity in the United States.

Three Gorges Dam

The Three Gorges Dam in China generates 22,500 megawatts of electricity. This is three times the electricity made by the Grand Coulee Dam in the United States. The Three Gorges Dam is 607 feet (185 m) high and 1.4 miles (2.3 km) wide. Its reservoir covers 400 square miles (1,036 sq km). To make the reservoir, more than 1,300 villages and 150 towns were flooded. One and a half million people had to move. The plant began operating in 2012. It made China the largest producer of hydropower in the world. Canada, Brazil, and the United States are the other top hydropower countries.

The new energy came quickly. Power plants were added to existing dams. These dams were used for irrigation and flood control before the war. With the extra power, the United States supplied the Allies' needs. After the fighting ended, the factories that produced war supplies changed to building products for the home.

Powering the Rest of the World

Hydropower remains an important source of electricity in the

United States. But it has not grown as much as other types of power.

In the rest of the world, hydropower is growing quickly. Countries with hills and mountains have rivers that rush down slopes. This means they can make electricity from hydropower. They benefit from this clean, reliable source of energy. The electricity these plants generate helps to fuel growth in cities and countries around the globe.

FURTHER EVIDENCE

Chapter Two offers information about how hydroelectric power made life easier for farmers in the Tennessee Valley. Identify a point the author makes about the TVA. What evidence does the author provide to support this point? The website below discusses life before the TVA. Find a quote on this website that supports the main point you identified. Does this quote support an existing piece of evidence in the chapter? Or does it offer a new piece of evidence?

Life Before TVA
mycorelibrary.com/hydroelectric-energy

CHAPTER THREE

THE POWER OF FALLING WATER

Hydroelectric power plants transform the energy of falling water into electric energy. Water has potential energy when it is above the surface of the earth. The pull of gravity gives it this energy. Water also has kinetic energy. This is the energy of motion. Water has kinetic energy when it falls or flows. For water to flow or fall, there must be

Gravity pulls water toward the center of the planet, giving that water the energy of motion.

a drop in elevation. Hydroelectric power plants are located in places where elevation changes.

In hydroelectric plants, the kinetic energy of falling water turns to mechanical energy when the water spins the turbine. A generator turns the mechanical energy into electrical energy. The amount of power that can be generated depends on the distance water falls. This distance is called the head. The power also depends on the speed of the water, which results from the slope of the ground downstream. This speed is called the flow.

Hydropower Plants

There are three types of hydroelectric power plants. The first are known as impoundment plants. These plants use dams to make electricity. They have a high head. A dam is built across a river. It blocks most of the river's flow, creating a reservoir. But a small part of the river's water is channeled around it. This small part is what will remain of the river. Electricity from impoundment dams is dependable. They work well

Some large dams, such as Hoover Dam in the United States, have many enormous generators.

even in times of drought. Power can be released quickly from reservoirs when electricity is needed.

Diversion plants are a second type of plant. Another name for them is run-of-the-river plants. They may use a small dam to create a head. Or they may use no dam at all. In diversion plants, a part of the river is run through a canal or a tube. This water spins the turbines. Normally, water falls between

Types of Dams

There are several types of dams. The shape and material used to build the dam depends on where it is built. Concrete gravity dams are built of huge concrete blocks. They lie straight across narrow gorges on river valleys. Buttresses, or braces, can be used to make a dam stronger. Arch dams curve upstream. They have supports on each end. They are built on rivers between rock walls. Embankment dams are made of packed earth. They are built across wide streams.

4 and 5 feet (1.2–1.5 m). Diversion plants are not flexible. They cannot store water to be released when electricity is needed.

The third type of hydroelectric plant is a pumped storage plant. These plants use two reservoirs at different heights. The two reservoirs may be close, or they may be miles away. Water falls from the higher reservoir through tubes and into turbines. It generates electricity. It then flows to the lower reservoir. When demand for electricity is low, the water from the lower reservoir is pumped back up. It can be used to make electricity again. Pumped

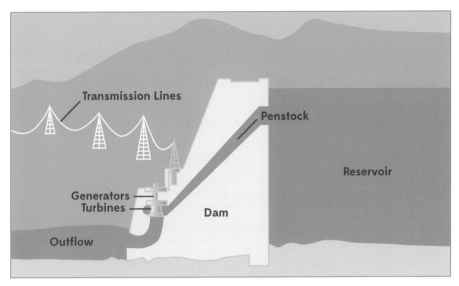

How a Hydroelectric Dam Works
A hydropower dam uses the force of falling water to move turbines. The turbines spin a generator and create electricity. Why do you think the dam is bigger at the bottom than at the top? How might the placement of the turbine affect the amount of electricity produced?

storage plants recycle the water. They do not release it downriver. These plants are very flexible.

The Power Plant

To make electricity, falling water runs down tubes called penstocks. The water may be from a dam, a river, or a stream. At the end of the penstock, the rushing water turns a turbine. The turbine is a propeller-like wheel. It is attached to a shaft or rod.

The water's energy makes the turbine spin like a pinwheel in the wind.

On the other side of the shaft, a large magnet surrounds a coil of wire. This is the generator. When the magnet spins, it causes an electrical current to flow in the coil. This generates electricity.

After the water does its job, it is released down a channel below the dam. This channel is called a tailrace. From there, the water returns to the river or falls to another reservoir to be reused.

Clean, Cheap, and Renewable

Hydroelectric power is clean. Unlike with fossil fuels, nothing is burned to generate electricity. The water and turbines release no harmful gases.

It is also the least expensive type of electricity. Water is free. Unlike oil and coal, it does not have to be dug out of the ground. Dams and power plants are expensive to build, but they can last a long time. In addition, the costs to produce electric power are low.

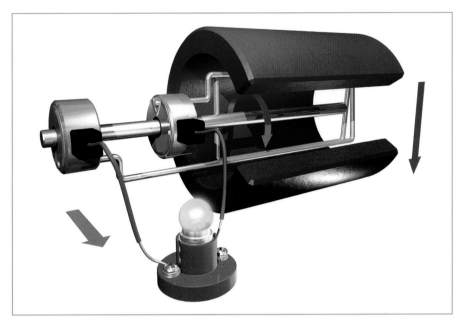

How a Generator Works

The shaft of the turbine in a hydropower plant is attached to a coil of wire. As the turbine turns, the coil of wire turns inside a magnet. Spinning the coil inside the magnet makes electrons move in the wire. It changes the energy of motion to electric energy. It generates electricity. What other ways can you think of to create spinning motion that a generator could turn into electricity?

The water that generates electricity is not used up. After it does its job, it returns to the river or stream. It becomes part of the water cycle again. Storing water in a reservoir with a dam helps make hydropower a dependable source of electricity.

Hydroelectricity can be released onto the grid in seconds. It can help out if demand for power spikes.

It can be used to fill in for wind and solar power if the wind doesn't blow or the sun doesn't shine. It can also be used as a backup when other types of power are disabled.

Environmental Costs

There are some problems with hydropower. When dams create reservoirs, towns may be flooded. In some countries, the government forces people to leave their homes. Reservoirs can also destroy animals' habitats. Archeological sites may be buried. Native hunting and fishing areas can vanish.

The plants and soil buried in the reservoir rot. When they rot, they give off methane. This gas can build up in the atmosphere. It can trap the sun's heat, warming the planet's climate over time. In most cases, gas is only released for a short time after the dam is built. Hydropower emissions are much lower than those from burning fossil fuels.

Dams reduce the flow of water downstream. Fish below the dam have to adapt. They must live with less

The environmental problems of dams result from the reservoirs they create and the flow of water they block.

water than normal. The water that passes through the turbines is cold. Cold water carries less oxygen. Fish need warm water and oxygen to live. They must adapt to living on less oxygen. Some fish cannot survive.

Dams can also prevent salmon and steelhead trout from freely swimming up the river. These fish usually swim back to where they were born to lay their eggs. Their numbers have decreased in many areas. The Columbia River flows in the northwest United States. In the 1800s, the river system had between

Ghost Town

Saint Thomas, Nevada, was a small town founded in 1865. It was located where the Muddy and Virgin Rivers met. In 1935 Saint Thomas was flooded to make Lake Mead, the reservoir for Hoover Dam. Townspeople were forced to abandon their homes. The town remained under at least 60 feet (18 m) of water for many years. Because of drought in the early 2000s, the lake level has dropped. Since 2012, the ruins have been exposed. Tourists now visit the ghost town.

10 and 16 million fish. Many dams were built in the area in the 1900s. By 2001 the number of fish had decreased to about 1.5 million.

In the United States, the government has made laws to help prevent more environmental damage. However, not all nations have rules like this. Some countries have built hydroelectric plants that have caused severe problems with their rivers and wildlife. It is up to the world's governments to create laws to make sure hydropower does as little harm to the environment as possible.

This address was given by Secretary of the Interior Harold Ickes on September 30, 1935, to dedicate Hoover Dam:

> *I venture to hope that this dam, with its great storage of health and wealth and happiness for thousands of people, will stand as a definite opening of a new era with respect to the natural resources of America; an era of conservation, which means the prudent use of all our natural resources for the greatest good of the greatest number of our people; an era that will recognize the principle that the riches of forest and mine and water were not bestowed by God to be ruthlessly exploited in order to enhance the wealth of a small group of rugged individualists, but were beneficently given to us as an endowment to be carefully used for the benefit of all the people.*

Source: Kevin Wehr. America's Fight Over Water.
New York: Routledge, 2004. Print. 101.

What's the Big Idea?

Take a close look at this passage. In 1935 the United States was still in the middle of the Great Depression. What is the main connection the secretary makes between the building of the dam and the welfare of the country? What is the goal of this speech? Is he trying to convince his listeners of something?

CHAPTER FOUR

THE FUTURE OF HYDROPOWER

The United States needs more electricity. So does the world. Today's digital devices and other technologies need power to run. By 2030, the United States is expected to use at least four times more power than in 2012. Some of this new power will come from water. The trick will be to make hydropower even greener than it has been.

Modern cities require huge amounts of electricity to keep up with demand.

Small- and medium-scale hydroelectric plants have less of an environmental impact than very large ones.

More Hydropower

There are possible sites for more than 5,000 new hydropower plants in the United States. These will not be large plants, like Hoover Dam or the Grand Coulee Dam. Sites for such big plants are no longer available. But even with smaller sites, the nation can still double its hydropower output. Small power plants can be used to provide cheap power to small communities. These will most likely be low-head projects.

Another way to increase power is to add more turbines and generators to existing plants.

Hydropower equipment can also be added to dams that are now used only for irrigation and flood control.

Many new hydropower sites are available in other countries. This source of electricity will continue to grow. It can bring electrical power and a modern lifestyle to rural areas around the world.

Cutting Down on Bad Effects

Hydropower's bad effects can be reduced with careful study and planning. New dams can be built so water is released from higher levels. This water will be warmer. Aerators

Hydropower in Bhutan

Bhutan is a small country. It sits at the foot of the Himalayas, a mountain range in Asia. People in Bhutan have long lived and farmed in rural communities. For many years, they had little technology. Today, Bhutan is using hydroelectricity to improve its people's lives. Its location in the mountains means it has large changes in elevation. This makes the area great for hydropower. In fact, the country generates more electricity than it can use. It sells the extra power to India.

Taking Care of Salmon

Salmon are born in rivers. As adults, they live in the ocean. They return to the rivers to lay their eggs. Dams stop their migrations up and down the river.

To help fish, hydroelectric plants can add channels that avoid the dams. The young fish can use the channels to swim downstream. Fish ladders allow the fish to move upstream. These are stepped pools around the dam. Fish locks can do the same. In some cases, fish are trucked around the dam. These measures can help reduce the impact of the dam on the salmon life cycle.

can be added to dams. These devices add more oxygen to the water when it rejoins the river. Dam builders can also find ways to allow fish to swim up and down the river. Taking these steps can help keep fish healthy.

Flooding large areas to make reservoirs cannot always be avoided. But the way it is done can change. People can be paid fairly for having to move. Care can be taken with wildlife. Plant material that gives off methane could be removed before the

Structures called fish ladders make it possible for fish to bypass dams.

Hydroelectric power will play an important role in creating a clean energy future.

area is flooded. This can reduce methane emissions. Taking these steps may cost more money. But it will help make hydropower a cleaner, fairer source of electricity.

The Future

Hydroelectricity made life better in the Tennessee Valley in the 1930s. It can do the same thing for countries all around the world today. It is a way to help poor countries leap forward.

In the United States, it will help meet the exploding demand for electricity and reduce the need for fossil fuels. Hydropower is cheap, flexible, renewable, reliable, and sustainable. It is one of the top alternative energy sources available today.

EXPLORE ONLINE

Chapter Four discusses the future of hydroelectric power. The website below features an article about this topic. It brings up the challenges that climate change will bring to hydropower. What new information can you find in this article? Does it change the way you think about hydroelectricity's future?

Climate Change Evaporates Part of China's Hydropower
mycorelibrary.com/hydroelectric-energy

FAST FACTS

- Hydropower is the oldest type of power other than that generated by humans and animals.
- In 2015 hydropower was responsible for 6 percent of all the electricity used in the United States.
- Generating electricity with hydropower is much cleaner than using fossil fuels.
- Water is renewed by the water cycle. It is a natural renewable resource.
- Hydroelectric power is flexible. It can be turned on and off in seconds. It is also reliable. Water can be stored behind dams to be released as needed.
- Often, rural and remote areas can be served more effectively with hydropower than with other types of power.
- Lakes made by hydropower dams can also be used for irrigation, flood control, storage of drinking water, and recreation.

- Hydropower has some problems. When dams are built, people and animals are displaced. Methane gas may be produced by rotting plant and animal material in the reservoir area. Fish may be blocked from migrating.
- Efforts are being made to reduce the impact of hydropower plants on the environment.

STOP AND THINK

Another View

This book talks about the Three Gorges Dam. As you know, every source is different. Ask a librarian or another adult to help you find another source about this structure. Consider whether the pain to displaced families was worth the benefits of controlling floods on the river. What is the point of view of the new source's author? How is it similar to or different from the point of view of this book's author?

You Are There

This book discusses the history of electricity. Imagine yourself at one of the world's first hydroelectric plants. Write a letter home describing the first time you saw a city with electric lights powered by hydropower. Tell your friends about what this meant to you. Be sure to add plenty of detail to your description.

Tell the Tale

Chapter Two of this book discusses the effect of the Tennessee Valley Authority. The TVA brought electricity to people who did not have it before. Imagine yourself living without electricity. What would your life be like? Write 200 words about how you would have fun if you did not have electricity.

Dig Deeper

After reading this book, what questions do you still have about whether hydroelectric power is safe for the environment? With an adult's help, find a few reliable sources that can help you answer your questions. Write a paragraph about what you learned.

GLOSSARY

aerator
a device that adds oxygen to water

conduit
a channel through which something passes

diversion
moving aside or going around

drought
dry conditions that result from a lack of rain

elevation
the height of a landform

gravity
a force that pulls objects toward the center of Earth

kinetic energy
the energy an object has because of its motion

methane
a gas given off when natural matter rots

patent
a license from the government to be the only person or company allowed to make a new invention

potential energy
the energy an object has because of its position

renewable
something that does not run out

rural
in the country, away from large cities

LEARN MORE

Books

Halls, Kelly Milner. *The Story of the Hoover Dam*. Ann Arbor, MI: Cherry Lake Publishing, 2014.

Parker, Steve. *Electricity*. New York: DK, 2013.

Ward, Sarah E. *Electricity in the Real World*. Minneapolis, MN: Abdo Publishing, 2013.

Websites

To learn more about Alternative Energy, visit **booklinks.abdopublishing.com**. These links are routinely monitored and updated to provide the most current information available.

Visit **mycorelibrary.com** for free additional tools for teachers and students.

INDEX

ABOUT THE AUTHOR

Terry Catasús Jennings is the author of many books for children. Her articles have appeared in the *Washington Post*, *Long Island News Day*, and *Ranger Rick*. She and her husband live in Northern Virginia.